D1745599

THE LONDON FILE
PAPERS FROM THE INSTITUTE OF EDUCATION

THE ARTS 5-16: CHANGING THE AGENDA

JOHN WHITE

INSTITUTE OF
EDUCATION
UNIVERSITY OF LONDON

Published by

the Tufnell Press

THE LONDON FILE - PAPERS FROM THE INSTITUTE OF EDUCATION

PUBLISHED
by
the Tufnell Press
47, Dalmeny Road, London, N7 0DY

First published 1992

BRITISH LIBRARY CATALOGUING-IN-PUBLICATION DATA
A catalogue record for this book is available from the British Library

ISBN 1 872767 06 0

Book design by Fiona Barlow, Carter Wong, London
Printed in Great Britain by Da Costa Print, London

CONTENTS

THE ARTS 5-16: CHANGING THE AGENDA

THE LONDON FILE - PAPERS FROM THE
INSTITUTE OF EDUCATION
Titles in the series include:

What place should the arts have in education? Traditionally, schools have taught English literature, art and music, and sometimes also drama and dance. Especially in secondary schools, these have been usually taught in isolation from each other, each the province of experts professionally attached to their particular art and to fellow-participants rather than to the arts as a whole. The 1988 National Curriculum has reinforced this traditional pattern by making art and music foundation subjects and by including literature within the foundation subject of English.

A result of this lack of communication between the arts subjects has been that the role of the arts in general in education has too little been considered. This is unfortunate. One might have expected policy-making in this area to begin with broader questions about what an education in the arts might hope to accomplish and only then to move to more specific questions about which arts should be pursued and in what ways. We have grown used to confining our thinking within specific categories which have been with us for a century and more.

In the late 1980s, however, things began to change. The work of *The Arts in Schools* project, begun by the School Curriculum Development Committee in 1985 and completed under the auspices of the National Curriculum Council in 1989, has recently been published. Its theoretical framework is found in *The Arts 5-16: A Curriculum Framework* (NCC, 1990). What is refreshing is the project's interest in looking at the arts as a whole and its recommendation that school curriculum planning in the arts should begin from this global perspective and only then go on into questions of what place visual, literary, musical and other artistic activities should play within the wider framework. In addition, despite its conservatism, the 1988 National Curriculum may help, unexpectedly, to focus attention on the arts as a whole. The clear priority it has given to literacy, mathematics and science may encourage teachers of humanities – including the arts – to cleave together in defence of their broad area. One goal of this paper is to help teachers of the arts to feel more closely involved in a common purpose, thus pushing forward the pioneering work of *The Arts 5-16* project.

But the paper is not only addressed to teachers of the arts, and perhaps not primarily so. Its main concerns, as is appropriate, are with fundamental questions about the aims of education in the arts and the broad ways in which these aims might be realised. Its first audience, therefore, should be those who make policy about the content of education and its aims.

The main message to policy-makers and teachers is that these questions about aims and their realisation are *difficult* to answer. *The Arts 5-16* recommendations, ground-breaking though they are, oversimplify the topic, producing neat, formally satisfying answers where only incomplete and untidy ones can reasonably be expected at this stage.

The paper begins with a critical discussion of *The* Arts 5-16 proposals on these lines; and continues with some first steps towards a more satisfactory alternative.

I

Where I part company with the *The Arts 5-16* proposal is over what I see as a misplaced egalitarianism in the way it proceeds. Let me explain.

(i) BALANCE AND EQUALITY

The notions of equality and of balance figure prominently in the account. They are found in the discussion of three central issues, to do with: (1) the arts *vis-à-vis* other curriculum areas; (2) the arts *vis-à-vis* each other; and (3) artistic activities (creating, appraising, etc.) *vis-à-vis* each other.

On (1), we read 'An education which aims to develop the full range and power of young people's intellectual abilities will certainly emphasise mathematics, science and verbal reasoning. It will also give equal weight to the arts.' (para 75). This echoes the position taken in the Gulbenkian

Report *The Arts in Schools* (1982), out of which the present project grew. Gulbenkian says 'The arts are crucial elements in a balanced curriculum: not more, not less, but certainly as important as other forms of knowledge'.

As for (2), we find that 'Provision should be balanced between the arts.... equal provision should be made for each of the major modes of artistic activity...' (para 88).

And on (3), 'The emphasis on arts teaching in all disciplines is often on promoting pupils' own creative work. We will argue that, for particular reasons, the best practice in primary as well as in secondary schools gives equal weight to developing young people's critical understanding of other people's work and their knowledge of different cultural practices and traditions.' (para 8). Again, 'There should be balance in the teaching of the arts between pupils' creative work and their critical understanding of the work of other people.' (para 93).

There is, finally, a further claim about equality. The paper distinguishes four elements of learning in the arts: (a) concepts, (b) skills, (c) attitudes and values, and (d) information. It argues 'that a balanced arts education will give equal weight to all of these' (para 142).

How are we to take these calls for balance, for equal weight and equal provision? There is a literal interpretation, based on the image of a weighing machine in which the scale-pans are in balance when they are of equal weight. On this view, the document would be claiming the same curricular provision (a) for the arts as a whole as compared with other comparable areas; (b) for specific forms of art; (c) for specific artistic activities within each form.

There are problems here, to which we will be returning, about how one identifies the elements in the different scale pans. In (a), for instance, how do we identify the other curriculum areas with which the arts as a whole are being compared, and with which they are said to be on an equal footing? Leaving these aside, what reason might be given for this equal weighting of elements in (a), (b) and (c)? *The Arts 5 to 16* report does not provide any rationale: it seems to take balance and equality as self-evidently desirable, without feeling the need to justify them.

But perhaps we are not expected to take these claims literally. Robert Dearden, in an excellent chapter on 'Balance and Coherence' in his book *Theory and Practice in Education*, suggests that appeals to balance in writings on the curriculum 'are often closely connected with justice, taken as meaning giving what is due' (pp. 62-3). What the report may have in mind is that in each area (a), (b) and (c) something has not been given its due and this should be rectified. In (a) the arts have had short shrift as against, say mathematics and the sciences; in (b) art forms like drama and dance have been poor relations to the verbal and visual arts and music; in (c) critical understanding of others' work has been put in the shade by the promotion of creative work. These are certainly prominent themes in the report and it may be that it is not advocating a mathematical carving up of the curriculum into equal sections, but a more general ethical rendering of what is due.

If we follow this interpretation it is understandable why no justification is given of the claims to do with balance and equality. If these boil down to the ethical demand that things should be given their due, then who could quarrel with that?

The second interpretation thus cuts no ice. We can agree with it at a general level, but it fails to answer the question 'What is it to give the things it is talking about their due?' When we apply this, as in (c), to critical understanding, then *just how important* is this as compared with creative work? Should the latter be reduced to a minimum? Should changes not go as far as this? In (b), *just how important* is dance, say, *vis-à-vis* painting or literature? Such questions are simply not addressed.

According to which interpretation one takes, therefore, the report is either calling for mathematical equality across the board, but not giving any justification for this; or it is making an acceptable but vacuous ethical statement. Its sub-title is 'A Curriculum Framework'. Certainly a curriculum framework is just what those attracted by a holistic approach to the arts in schools require; but, unless we follow the unsubstantiated mathematical interpretation, the report fails to deliver its promised goods.

Still, it has given us something. It has focused our attention on the arts in schools as a whole. Its claims about balance and equality under (a), (b) and (c) provoke important questions which, even if not satisfactorily answered within the report itself, cry out for further investigation. If the arts as a whole are to claim their rightful due in the curriculum as against other areas, on what basis can they do this? Are there priorities of educational importance among the specific artistic areas, or are they all equally important? How important is critical understanding of others' works as an objective as compared to creative work?

(ii) ELEMENTS OF COMPARISON

These are big questions. To answer them would take at least a book. In the rest of Part I, I will only be able to focus on one major issue. A broader canvas will come with Part II.

Still keeping within the helpful (a)-(b)-(c) framework, in each of these three areas we need to say more about the *elements* being compared with one another. When we ask how important the arts as a whole are compared with other things, what are these other things? When we wonder about priorities among specific art forms, how are we to identify these? How are we to map the different activities within each form? The Gulbenkian Report gives us a way into (a) and *The Arts 5-16* into (b) and (c), so we can make a start with these.

(a) The arts *vis-à-vis* other curricular areas

What are we comparing here? In claiming that 'the arts are ...not more, nor less, but certainly as important as other forms of knowledge', the Gulbenkian Report follows Hirst's (1965) theory of a liberal education based on a number of logically discrete forms of knowledge. One of these is 'literature and the fine arts'. If Hirst is right, then one can see how an argument may be mounted in favour of equal provision for the artistic form of knowledge and each one of the other six or seven forms. There are well-known difficulties in Hirst's theory, not least in its claim that the arts constitute a form of knowledge. I will not go into these here; but will merely make the more general point that the chances of being able to provide a neat taxonomy in which the arts have some kind of equal status with a limited number of other elements seem slim indeed. This applies to the well-known taxonomy in the HMI Report, *Curriculum 11-16* (HMI, 1977), where 'the aesthetic and the creative' is one of eight equally important 'areas of experience'. Despite the somewhat nostalgic attachment many schools and LEAs have to the areas of experience these days, hoping to find in them some more liberal framework than that of the excessively subject-centred National Curriculum, they should be reminded that no good reasons have been provided to justify this taxonomy and therewith the attractively convenient basis for curriculum planning which it provides. The general point also applies to the view in *The Arts 5-16* that the arts are equal in importance to mathematics, science or verbal reasoning. Why should we assume this? If we take particular comparisons, like that between the arts and mathematics, we should surely keep an open mind about their relative importance until we have heard supporting arguments. It may be, for all we know, that the arts are of considerably less educational value than mathematics – or considerably more. We cannot judge until we have explored all the complexities of this topic. We will come back to this later.

(b) The arts *vis-à-vis* each other

The Arts 5-16 claims that there should be equal provision 'for each of the major forms of artistic activity'. What does it take these to be and why? It claims (para 55) that there are five different 'modes of understanding' in the arts : the visual, the aural, the kinaesthetic, the verbal, the enactive. These are found cross-culturally, unlike the more conventional division which we find in our schools into music, dance, drama, the visual and the verbal arts. The latter is a culture-bound classification. Items on the second list can fall under more than one heading on the first list: drama, for instance, involves the verbal as well as the enactive mode; dance, the aural and the visual as well as the kinaesthetic.

There are several problems here. First a specific one. The division into modes of understanding seems to exclude architecture, or at least aspects of architecture. It would seem partly to fall under the visual mode – 'using light, colour and images'. But architects use more than these. Despite the claim that the fivefold division into modes is not culture-bound, it is hard to see it otherwise than as derivative from the conventional culture of the school, in which painting has a hallowed place, but not architecture.

A second problem is more general and goes deeper. It is claimed that the arts rest on distinct artistic modes of understanding. What is it that is being understood in these different domains? In what way is art productive of understanding? Light is thrown on this by the discussion in paragraphs 51-56. 'The arts', we are told, 'emerge from the fundamental human capacity for making sense of experience by representing it in symbolic form' (para 51). This general capacity is multifaceted. The most obvious example is verbal language, in that we use words 'to symbolise ideas and events' (para 52). But 'verbal language enables us to formulate some ideas but not others' (para 54). 'For these we use other modes of understanding such as mathematics or music or visual images' (ibid.).

This is an intellectualist account of the arts, which, as in Hirst's theory, seeks to assimilate them to forms of knowledge like mathematics and science. Will it do? That depends on how far the notion of symbolic understanding can be extended beyond the sphere of verbal symbols. It is true that here we can make the distinction mentioned in the document between symbol and idea. We have the word, the verbal symbol 'cat'. Lying behind it, and expressed by it, we have the idea or concept cat, expressed in other languages by the symbols 'chat', 'Katze', 'koshka', etc. Falling under the concept cat we have, finally, (in the case of this concept) particular cats which instantiate the concept. So we have a threefold division between the realm of words, the realm of concepts and features of the world picked out by those concepts. Understanding comes into this account in that to understand the meaning of a word, we have to understand the underlying concept, and in that, for many concepts directly and for all concepts indirectly, we can only understand them by relating them to our experience of features of the world: we could not be said to have grasped the concept cat adequately, for instance, unless we had some kind of experience of particular cats.

So much for verbal symbols and ideas. Can this sort of account be extended to the arts in their different forms? Does it enable us to identify five modes of artistic understanding – visual, aural, kinaesthetic, verbal, enactive? Symbols certainly do exist in the aural area. There are musical symbols, which can be written verbally, like 'crotchet', or non-verbally. These symbols express concepts – the concept of a crotchet, of repeating a passage from the beginning, or whatever. And these concepts are instantiated in experience: particular examples of one-unit time intervals or of repetitions fall under them. In this way, musical symbols are not only *like* verbal symbols: they *are* verbal symbols or are translatable into them. If we are looking for other types of symbolic understanding beyond the verbal, as *The Arts 5-16* suggests, then we must start at a different point.

In any case, music is something of a special case in being based on a symbolic structure. In visual art, for instance, we do not find a parallel: painters do not compose scores. We are looking for a notion of symbolic forms which applies across the board. And it must be a notion in which, as with verbal symbols, one can make the distinction between symbol and expressed idea; and in which the expressed idea is related to experience, in that it helps us 'to make sense of experience'.

What, then, could count as visual or aural symbols and ideas? Perhaps we should take a work of art itself to be a symbol. On this view the New World Symphony or the Mona Lisa would each be symbols. Each would be expressing an idea, the former a peculiarly musical idea and the latter a peculiarly visual idea, neither of which could be expressed in any other medium. What can we say about these ideas? If the parallel with verbal symbols (like 'cat') is to go through, the ideas are general concepts, capable of multiple instantiation in experience. But this is hard to make sense of in the arts. Shall we say that the New World Symphony is a symbol of the idea of a subtle kind of ineffable nostalgia? And can we then treat this as a general idea which can be instantiated in different ways? One trouble here is that the Symphony itself then seems to come out as one of these instantiations, whereas it should come out as a symbol (i.e., pursuing the cat analogy, it starts off as parallel to the word 'cat', but seems to end up as parallel to a particular cat). But a more substantial consideration is that to see works of art as symbolising general ideas is to ignore the role that their particularity plays in our experience of them. We enjoy the New World Symphony as something unique, as something brought into the world with its own peculiar and irreplaceable features. We do not look behind it to some concept or collection of concepts to which it directs us. Works of art have often been compared with people with whom we are intimately connected. Enjoying the company of a lover or a friend is to enjoy being with this individual person with this unique constellation of characteristics which makes him what he is. So it is with our experience of art.

If we eschew general ideas, we should also abandon the thought that works of art, via the ideas they express, help us to 'make sense of experience'. In everyday life, we can make sense of the inchoate experience we would otherwise have of the world only because we have concepts like 'cat', 'red', 'three' and the like which impose on it some structure. If what has been said of the arts is correct, they cannot perform an analogous function. Music and painting do not make sense of experience: they themselves embody ways in which strictly delimited areas of our experienced world – e.g. those within the framework of a symphony or painting – are organised for our contemplation.

If the arts *did* as a rule give us access to ideas which made sense of our experience, the purpose of our looking at pictures and listening to musical works would be to extend our understanding. But talk of 'modes of understanding', as found in *The Arts 5-16*, is misleading. It assimilates the arts too closely to what are undoubtedly kinds of understanding, like history, science or mathematics. This view of the arts fails to give a convincing account of why we repeatedly go back to favourite works. We do not typically do this because we have forgotten what we once understood and now wish to be reminded of it. Neither do we typically do so to enlarge our understanding of the world, to find things out about it that we did not know before. In-so-far as we enjoy re-experiencing works of art *as* works of art, we do so in some ways as we enjoy meeting and re-meeting old friends: for the pleasures and other feelings – of different sorts, to be sure – that they evoke in us, for the attractions of their irreplaceable individuality.

None of this is to deny that the arts *can* deepen our understanding of the world or help us to make sense of our experience. Literature can certainly do this – and in more than one way. We can get a good picture of early nineteenth century aristocratic life in Russia from *War and Peace*. Literature, especially novels, can be viewed purely as a resource to provide historical, sociological and psychological knowledge of a sort that non-aesthetic enquiries could have furnished. This is also true of some paintings. But literature, especially poetry, can also, or so I would argue, deepen our understanding not least of ourselves in ways which are part of our aesthetic engagement with the work. This is also true of some other works of art. I will come back to this in Part II. The main point I want to make now is that the fact that some works do deepen our understanding of the world is not enough to show that all do, or that it is right to see the arts essentially as 'modes of understanding'. Neither is it the case that the aesthetically-based understanding we get especially from poetry comes via symbols more esoteric than the words of the poem, i.e. via peculiarly aesthetic symbols, expressing ideas in the manner claimed by *The Arts 5-16*.

This lengthy discussion of the role of symbols and ideas sprang out of the key contention in *The Arts 5-16* that the arts curriculum should be subdivided according to the five distinct modes of understanding in the arts, for each of which equal provision should be made. My counter-argument has been that this whole approach to subdividing the arts is radically incoherent. It is ironic that a document whose main intention has been to strengthen the position of the arts in the school curriculum should model them so closely on those disciplines concerned with the pursuit of truth and underplay their own uniqueness.

As to what the elements *should* be into which the arts curriculum should be subdivided, I do not want to come out with a definitive list here. Constructing such a list would need to take into account a number of considerations and different people might weight these differently. I'll restrict myself to a few remarks only. First, I would urge looking initially not to *theory* – e.g. to the epistemological theorising found in the document about modes of understanding, but to the *practices* of art with which we are already familiar in our culture or cultures, understanding 'practice' here in MacIntyre's (1981) sense of a 'coherent and complex form of socially established co-operative human activity through which goods internal to that form of activity are realised' (p 175). There will be no tidy list of artistic practices, although we can isolate major areas, each the focus for a number of sub-practices, to do with such things as painting and drawing, sculpture, pottery, instrumental music, song, opera, poetry, drama, fiction, film, dance, architecture, urban planning. (Beyond these we might think of applied arts like furniture-making, embroidery, various kinds of designing.) Another desideratum is catholicity. If we want children to get inside the arts as a form of social life, we would do well to keep their horizons as broad as possible – to give them a picture of all art's manifold components, bearing in mind that the concept of art is radically contestable and that people would draw lines around it in different places. Pupils should not be steered towards a specific, limited conception of what counts as art – e.g. one which includes classical music but excludes jazz or popular songs, or one which cuts out the applied arts, but should be left with the openness to entertain alternative conceptions. Cutting across this last consideration, and to be weighed against it, is the proposition that the extent to which different branches of art are to have a place in the curriculum depends first on an overall picture of educational aims and the place of specifically aesthetic aims within this, secondly on the contribution which the school as distinct from other institutions like the family or the media can make towards the latter, and third on the role of the timetabled curriculum as distinct from other aspects of the school's life and ethos. These are all big topics and I do no more than mention them here. We will be coming back to some of them in Part II.

One of the reasons why *The Arts 5-16* looks to its five modes of understanding is that it wants to avoids a culture-bound view of the arts. Its chief target here is ethnocentrism, in the shape of privileging traditional categorisations of the arts in mainstream British culture over minority ethnic perceptions. Large issues arise at this point about what weight should be given to mainstream values of all kinds, ethical as well as aesthetic. There should be no automatic assumption that all cultures should be treated equally: there is no short cut to going patiently through arguments of some complexity. But suppose we grant that at least some weight should be given to the art forms of minority cultures. It does not follow from this that we should look for a way of carving up the arts which is *culture-free*. I doubt whether such a thought makes sense. The answer to ethnocentrism is not culture-transcendence, but culture-rootedness in more than one culture. This goes back to the points made above about practices and about catholicity. Practices are located in cultures, not abstracted from them. The way forward is to begin from central practices in mainstream British culture, assuming – which some may contest – that all children are to live their lives to some extent as part of this larger society. To these should be added artistic practices from minority groups, partly in the interests of catholicity, partly for ethical reasons of equality of respect.

The argument in this section has underlined, once again, the complexity of the issues at stake and the inadvisability of trying to regiment them within a theoretical framework which promises neat, simple solutions but ends up in conceptual entanglements.

(c) Artistic activities *vis-à-vis* each other

Which elements *within* each art are to be equally weighted or at least given their due? *The Arts 5-16* contrasts 'creative work' with 'critical understanding of other people's work' (para 8). It also uses a distinction between 'making' and 'appraising' (para 112). 'Making' includes performing as well as painting, writing poems, etc. 'Appraising describes all the processes through which young people engage with existing work. This includes reflecting critically on their own work as well as on other people's work. We use the term appraising to suggest the need for critical judgement and discrimination' (para 114).

In this last quotation there is some uncertainty over whether what is being contrasted with making (in a sense which includes performance) is *any* kind of engagement with a work, including for instance contemplating a work or the activity of the imagination which may be embodied in such contemplation; or specifically critical reflection. The final sentence of the quotation points rather firmly towards the latter. This is by no means just a semantic point. It goes to the heart of what should be central in the arts curriculum and where the weight should fall between different kinds of pursuit. For the most part the general line of the document is that there should be a shift of emphasis away from creative activities (or making) and towards critical activities. The danger in dichotomising like this is that a third activity, engagement with works in the sense of looking at paintings, listening to music, reading poetry and so on, will be left out of account or seen merely as a necessary condition of, and thus subordinate to, critical reflection. This connects with the point made earlier about the over-intellectualised view of education in the arts that we find in this paper. Putting the weight on critical reflection brings the objectives of the arts curriculum closer – too close – to the ratiocinative objectives of other parts of the curriculum. It is a mistake to think that in order to be a pukka educational area the arts must show that they contribute to knowledge and

12

understanding, that they help children to reason, to provide ordered arguments for and against claims. In many people's minds education itself is essentially to do with the development of knowledge and understanding: this is its overarching aim. This belief may lie behind the proposals in the document. But it is highly contestable. An alternative view, for which I have argued elsewhere, is that the aims of education should be conceived more broadly, as to do with promoting the pupil's and others' well-being as self-determining persons. In this the cultivation of critical reasoning in different areas has an important place, but as a sub-aim, not as the whole story. The questions of which kinds of artistic activities should figure in the curriculum and of how they should be weighted need to be tackled from this more inclusive standpoint on the aims of education. I have given no argument as yet about the relative importance of what I shall call sensuous engagement with the arts – e.g. looking, listening, reading, merely drawn attention to the fact that it may get overlooked or subordinated to other ends.

II

The Arts 5-16 has raised, but not adequately answered, three central questions: (a) how important are the arts among curriculum activities? (b) what priorities of importance are there among the different arts? and (c) what priorities of importance are there among the different arts activities?

In formulating a whole-arts policy for schools all these questions need to be addressed. But as we have begun to see, we will not get very far in answering them before we tackle the larger question: what are the purposes of education in the arts? It points back, of course, to an even bigger question, about the purposes of education in general.

In the second half of this paper, I shall not try exhaustively to get to grips with these issues. I restrict myself, rather, to making the first steps to set a whole-arts policy on securer foundations, first by looking briefly at the purposes of arts education, and secondly, by relating this to the institutional means by which these purposes might best be attained. This will bring us back, as we shall see, to topics (a) (b) and (c). In the whole of this discussion I am aware that I shall be raising more questions than I can answer. But this is how things must be at this embryonic stage of the debate.

(A) THE PURPOSES OF EDUCATION IN THE ARTS

(1) Opening up options

It is widely agreed that a central feature of a liberal-democratic society such as our own is that its members should be self-determining individuals, whose well-being is dependent on their own autonomous choice of goals, rather than the latters' being ascribed for them by tradition or authority. This generates, as one important educational aim in such a society, acquainting each person with a wide range of goals from which he or she may select those they prefer. By 'goals' I have in mind both intrinsic and extrinsic objectives. An intrinsic objective is one which is pursued for its own sake, an extrinsic one, for the sake of something else. An example of an intrinsic goal might be walking in the country; of an extrinsic goal, working as a solicitor (in order to have a comfortable income). Many goals can have both intrinsic and extrinsic aspects: one may, for instance, choose to become a solicitor not only as a route to personal affluence, but also for its intellectual challenges.

Artistic activities figure in the wide range of goals just mentioned. Intrinsic activities include sensuous engagement with works of art – looking at pictures, reading poetry, listening to music. Extrinsic activities, likely also to have an intrinsic dimension to them, include various kinds of paid employment in the artistic field – as actor, member of a symphony orchestra, film cameraman, manufacturer of artists' materials, music critic. They also include various kinds of creative activities, which may or may not be paid, like writing poems or painting pictures. (I call creative activities 'extrinsic' because their central purpose is normally to produce a piece of work – a sonnet or a watercolour – and the artistic activities themselves are instrumental to that. This is not to deny, as I said above, that they can also, and at the same time, be pursued for their own sake).

14

In a liberal democracy every citizen's education will ideally acquaint him or her with a range of artistic activities, among other things. There are two points to make about this. First, nothing has been said about the *routes* by which people come to be acquainted with different activities. A person may become attracted to writing poetry having read a lot of other people's poetry: she might not have written any poetry herself, either in English classes at school, or privately. Secondly, there is nothing in this argument to say that artistic goals are more important than any other goals. They are on a par with countless other options: banking, watching TV soaps, gardening, selling food. This also means that, as far as this argument goes, there is no reason why everyone must adopt artistic goals, or, having adopted them, stick to them. They are merely options like everything else.

Yet among the various artistic options, one has often been singled out as of especial significance: sensuous engagement with works of art for its own sake. Harold Osborne (1986, pp 298-9) has argued on these lines, seeking to justify the 'expansion and enhancement of aesthetic sensibility' as an educational aim. This goes further than, but includes, a justification of engagement with the arts, since it also covers aesthetic experience of nature and of the human environment. Osborne sees the transition which our society is now undergoing, towards one in which work loses its old salience, as enabling the cultivation of 'cultural values' not only in a leisured elite but in the population as a whole. 'Culture' consists in the cultivation for their own sake of faculties originally developed for purposes of evolutionary survival like intelligence, intellectual curiosity and altruistic fellow-feeling. Another of these originally practical faculties is perception of the environment. In its intrinsic form it has become aesthetic experience: this is virtually definable as perception for its own sake.

Aesthetic experience is thus in the same category as the cultivated pursuit of intelligence in mathematics and logic, of intellectual curiosity in science and history, of religious awe and reverence in organised religion. The increasingly leisured individuals of the future will be able to devote themselves to one or more of such cultural activities. Will aesthetic concerns have any privileged place among them? On this Osborne states that 'aesthetic appreciation is the most important (cultural value) and has an even more general appeal than the acquisition of knowledge for its own sake' (p. 299). He does not say why it is the most important value. If he had done so, we might – it is not clear – have had a reason for making aesthetic experience an indispensable ingredient in human flourishing as distinct from an option which some might adopt and others ignore.

As it stands, Osborne's position points towards an educational justification of aesthetic engagement which consists in acquainting pupils with cultural pursuits among which they will later choose which they prefer. The arts would presumably be an important element within the wider field of the aesthetic because of their 'high cultural value' (p. 298), in that it is in aesthetic experience of works of art that perception for its own sake is most fully developed.

The importance which Osborne attaches to sensuous engagement with the arts in an increasingly leisured society is intuitively attractive, but as we have seen needs further argument. In addition this general claim needs to be distinguished from his more specific view of what constitutes this sensuous engagement. Aestheticians tend to divide into two broad camps – those who wish to restrict the domain of aesthetic experience to experience of certain formal properties of a work or – slightly more widely – of properties discernable by trained perception alone; and those for whom other qualities of a work – its expressive qualities, for instance, or its reflection of how things are in the world, are also included. On the first view, aesthetic experience is entirely autonomous, a *sui generis* form of perception that has nothing to do with anything outside the work; on the second, it has all sorts of links with the rest of our lives, with our feelings, thoughts, moral and spiritual concerns.

Osborne belongs to the first camp. For him aesthetic experience comes close to the exercise of our perceptual powers for their own sake. This would seem to imply that the aesthetic qualities of a work of art – or natural object – are confined to those which are perceptually discriminable. Cultivating a leisure-time interest in the arts is a matter of developing ever more skilful powers of discriminating such things as patterns of musical sound and their interrelationships, or connections and contrasts among lines, tones, spatial forms and colours in visual art.

On this view it is hard to see interest in the arts as anything more than an option on all fours with other things. Since the realm of the aesthetic is disconnected from other human concerns, those who do not choose to cultivate such connoisseurship need not feel that they are excluding themselves from something vital to their well-being – any more than they need feel this if they decide not to go in for chess or bacteriology.

On the second, wider, conception of aesthetic experience which is linked more closely with other human interests, the opening-up-options argument still applies, although the option in question is now more broadly conceived. Those who are drawn towards literature, music and the visual arts become absorbed by these not only for the increasingly fine discriminations which acquaintance with them brings, but also for their revelatory and expressive powers. Whether anyone would be missing out if they did not choose this kind of option but went in for athletics or the life of the gourmet is another question. We will leave it open for the time being.

So far we have been discussing only the aesthetic aspects of engaging with works of art. Even on the broader conception of the aesthetic, there are reasons why reading literature, looking at paintings and so on are of interest, which go beyond the aesthetic. Especially via literature, but also via other arts, one can enlarge one's understanding of social history, sociology and psychology. In choosing options, some people may be inclined towards the arts for extra-aesthetic, as well as aesthetic, reasons. As far as I can see, there is no basis here for arguing that *everybody* must weave artistic goals into their life: some people may not rate the enlargement of their understanding as important to them, or if they do, they may prefer to acquire the understanding by a different route.

Even though on none of the arguments given so far can we lay down that *everybody* would be better off if engagement with the arts were one of their goals in life, there are reasons to think that, if only this option were presented to them, *very many* people would be attracted to it. Osborne writes, as we have seen, that aesthetic appreciation has an even more general appeal than the acquisition of knowledge for its own sake. Without being confined to his narrow definition of the aesthetic, we can see why this might well be so. Whatever deeper significance they may (or may not) have, the arts first of all delight the senses, bewitching us by melody, contrasts of colour, vivid imagery. To pursue knowledge in physics and mathematics, in philosophy or history requires great and often painful intellectual effort, while experience of the arts is immediately pleasurable. This constitutes part of the reason why the arts have such a wide appeal. But one also needs to point to the many-facetedness of interest that works of art possess, amounting in the case of great works even to inexhaustibility. It is not surprising that once one becomes acquainted with the music of Beethoven or the plays of Shakespeare one wants to return to these time and time again, not only reacquainting oneself with old delights, but also uncovering new layers of meaning or perceiving new patterns as one proceeds. Almost effortlessly, as if by seduction, one finds oneself entering a rich new world of the senses and of the spirit, to explore which one knows not even a lifetime will suffice.

(2) Beyond options: further claims for the arts

A first purpose of education in the arts has therefore to do with the expansion of options. Can one go further and argue that continued engagement with art throughout one's life is a necessary condition of anyone's flourishing or that it has some social utility that would equally make it, ideally, a universal goal? Leaving aside any clearly non-aesthetic benefits of engagement with the arts, aesthetic experience of works of art in the wider sense has been variously said to help resolve psychological tensions and foster inner harmony; to help us to understand our own existence; to promote mutual sympathy and understanding; to break down feelings of isolation from the rest of mankind; to reinforce socially accepted values; to promote morality. Some writers see it as performing the redemptive role in society today which religion played in earlier times.

If valid, these claims provide educational justifications of some moment, although whether any of them are strong enough to take us beyond the opening-up-options justification is not something we should take for granted. We will be examining them in more detail in the rest of this section.

On a broader conception of the aesthetic, the objects of aesthetic experience are not limited to perceptible features, still less to such formal features as the complexity and unity in which sensuous phenomena – tones, colours, sounds – are bound together. The work of art is not, or is not always, an objective, completed entity, requiring only our trained aesthetic perception to yield its aesthetic fruit. On the contrary, for the latter to be possible, we must often make a contribution of our own in the shape of an imaginative involvement with the work which brings it to completion. On one such conception, that of R K Elliott, one role of imagination is to enable us to experience works 'from within', as if we were participants in their worlds, or were entering into intimate communion with the characters portrayed in them or with their creators. In these ways we experience works as delivering situations (as in painting) or as expressing emotion (as in music) or both (as in poetry) (Elliott, 1972, p 157).

If one conceives aesthetic experience as not only of perceptual, including formal features, but also, at least in many cases, of imagined human feelings and situations, this helps to provide a non-contingent link between aesthetics and other human interests. Educationally, it enables us to see cultivating in young people a love of art not only as opening up new options, but also as helping them to live a fuller human life.

Anthony O'Hear (1988) has recently discussed the wider value to us of engagement with the arts. He writes

> Art, on the other hand (i.e. unlike science), is intimately involved in our sense of the value of things. First, by means of its sympathetic re-enactments of anthropomorphic perspectives on the world, it can play a central role both in value enquiry and in coming to an understanding of the nature of one's own existence and the meanings available in it. And, then, through its ability to resolve, at least for a time, certain fundamental tensions in our existence, it is well fitted to play a role in fostering harmony in one's own existence. (pp. 162-3)

The first of these claims is that art promotes value-enquiry and self-understanding; the second that it resolves certain tensions and fosters harmony. Are they both sound?

(1) The first claim might seem to suggest that art is valuable to us for theoretical reasons, i.e. that it helps us to uncover truths with which we were not previously acquainted. It certainly can do this. In the field of value-enquiry, we can come to learn about the ethical values of other

cultures or sub-cultures or other historical periods through their art, especially through their literature. But putting things like this underrates the importance that the arts can play in our ethical life. It appears to make engaging with them instrumental to something else, the pursuit of knowledge; and to suggest that if non-aesthetic evidence about values were superior to that furnished by art, the latter might prove dispensable. In addition, it is not even clear that in order to attain these theoretical benefits, one needs to engage *aesthetically* with a work, as distinct from mining it, as a scholar, for the light it might shed on other things.

But perhaps O'Hear has other things in mind than theoretical enquiry. He also writes of the contribution art can make to self-knowledge, and self-knowledge is perhaps more a form of practical wisdom than a theoretical achievement. As David Hamlyn (1977) has implied, it can scarcely be modelled on forms of understanding, like science or mathematics, where a distinction can be drawn between the knowing subject and an independent known object. Knowing oneself better is to have got one's priorities more into order, to have come more clearly to see what concerns weigh with one more than others. It involves having dwelt not on one's scheme of values, or hierarchy of desires, as a whole – for this would take us back to the misconception of self-knowledge as confrontation with some kind of inspectable object; but on particular values and on conflicts between them. One role of art is to enable us to dwell on, or better, perhaps, to dwell in our values or desires and their associated emotions in this more particular and less global way. Since works of art are produced to be enjoyed by a public, the desires, emotions and conflicts among these which they express are typically those which many have experienced; and one mark of the greatness of a work is its ability to strike such chords in all of us. In aesthetic engagement with art we come to a profounder self-awareness, of ourselves as unique individuals and at the same time of ourselves as members of a particular community or culture, and as human beings in general. We come to dwell not only in what we *do* feel but also in what we *would* feel if our circumstances were different, or became different. Art both reinforces feelings and priorities we already have and also shakes them up, unsettles established patterns and allows us imaginatively to entertain alternatives – a state, for instance, where grief dominates over everything, or where murder no longer belongs to the unthinkable.

This kind of argument for the ethical import of art may be charged with turning it into a vehicle for moral improvement, and therein treating it just as instrumentally as it is treated in the claim, examined earlier, that art can help in theoretical value-enquiry. We have to tread carefully here. There is no suggestion in this context that through the arts we may come to possess values that we did not possess before, e.g. altruistic values where previously we were egoistical. It may or may not be true that art, or some art, can have this power: to determine this would require empirical investigation. The point to be made is not that engagement with the arts gives us *new* values – although it might do this, but that we have to bring to it desires, feelings and the values they enshrine, which we *already* possess.

It is because we bring to our experience of art concerns that we already possess in life that art can play an often-remarked role in binding us together. On Osborne's narrower view of aesthetic experience it could well nurture mutual understanding among the aesthetically initiated; but we now see how this circle can be both deepened and widened: deepened, because those who engage with a particular work of art can become conscious not only of a shared exercise of skills of discrimination but also of the shared life-emotions and values they bring to the work; and widened, because the sharing now goes beyond the initiated and includes others in society unacquainted with this work, or perhaps, indeed, with any works of art. The public character of works of art, their role as a focal point for shared experience, is from an ethical perspective an important feature of them. Since the ethical values which individuals possess come to them, often in complex ways (see Taylor, 1990), from the cultures and communities in which they live, art can help to bind us not only as fellow human beings, but also as members of more localised groups. As O'Hear puts it: 'through art, indeed, the individual can come to a powerful realisation of the truth of Bradley's claim that a community enters into his essence' (p. 148). This adds a further dimension to O'Hear's point about the role of art in fostering self-understanding. This mutual binding is not exclusively a matter of shared awareness; for experience of art, in encouraging us to dwell on the springs of our ethical life, recommits us to what we value, thereby strengthening their role in our life, both individually and communally. Savile (1982, p. 107), drawing on Hume, gives an interesting example: the tapering of pillars upwards from a broader base insensibly reinforces a shared desire for security.

21

In these ways, through common roots in our desires and emotions, art reflects and fosters our ethical life. It has not been proposed, so far at least, that all art does this. Music, and among it the greatest, can be aesthetically interesting for its patterns and complexities of sound, even when we do not hear it as expression. This said, it may still be the case that the patterns and complexities themselves are ethically relevant, but in a different way. We shall be taking up this point in the next section.

(2) O'Hear's second claim is that art can play a part in resolving certain fundamental tensions in our existence and thereby foster harmony. He has in mind such tensions as those between the self and the objective world, between feeling and reason, between the natural and the conventional, between the individual and the community. He writes of the redemptive powers of art, its ability to save us from 'gazing into the horrors of the night' (p. 140).

Elsewhere he makes a significantly different claim to do with tensions, that 'art can help us creatively to express and explore the tensions caused in us by the fundamental dualisms of our nature' (p. 148). Expressing and exploring tensions is different from resolving them. Can art do either?

Just what resolution means in O'Hear's context would need further exploration, but the claim that art resolves tensions would seem to depend on evidence which he does not provide. For him art seems to have powers once ascribed to religion – redemptive powers, as he puts it, of transforming our life from a meaningless jumble of conflicting elements into a harmonious unity. This may well bring art *too* close to religion. It suggests perfectibilism. The ideal of human perfectibility, as Passmore (1970) has reminded us, has deep roots in our history, not least in the history of our religious and political ideas, from ancient times, but is in his view to be shunned, not welcomed. 'To achieve perfection in any of its classical senses, as so many perfectibilists have admitted, it would first be necessary to cease to be human, to become godlike, to rise above the human condition' (p. 326).

Quite another outlook on human life sees conflict and tension as ineradicable from it. In contemporary ethics one sees this in writers like Williams (1985) who stress the irreducible diversity of values. From this perspective, O'Hear's second suggestion, that art helps us to express and explore basic tensions, may be more fruitful: it seems a surer vehicle of self-understanding than when viewed from the perfectibilist standpoint, since there it may lead us into a false conception of what we are.

At the same time, in any individual's life conflicts have to be managed somehow. Balances have to be struck, values weighted, all within some kind of personal system of psychological regulation. On this view of human flourishing, conflicts co-exist within a unitary framework, one which is constantly changing with experience as balances are struck in different places. This has its obvious parallel in the contrasting elements held together within the framework of a work of art. Like a self, a work of art is nothing fixed. Both are endlessly open to being seen from new perspectives, to new features coming to the fore while others recede. Art may speak to us not only in its sensuous delights and its links with our emotional life, but also in its mirroring of our psychic constitution as a whole. If this is on the right lines, then even the least expressive music may still be ethically important to us. Music, indeed, may be a more faithful mirror of ourselves than painting. In the latter, the whole work is laid before us simultaneously for our contemplation. But we never see ourselves at any one time as a complete entity; to think in this way is to resort to that misconceived notion of self-understanding with which we dealt above. Music, flowing through time, never graspable *in toto*, but only in more local stretches and contrasts, is closer to our self as we know it.

Perhaps, after all, O'Hear has something more like this, and not perfectibilism, in mind in writing about art's contribution to our inner harmony. If so, it would be better not to link this with talk of redemption and salvation. Art may indeed have replaced religion in our age as a central element in our flourishing and in our self-understanding; but what it can do for us should not be exaggerated: our lives are not in danger without art, only vastly poorer.

How far do these arguments show that the purposes of education in the arts cannot be restricted to enlarging options? Art can have a more intimate connection with our personal and collective flourishing – with fostering self-knowledge, reinforcing our ethical values, binding us together as members of communities. In this way it is not simply on a par with abseiling, do-it-yourself or other options. At the very least an education in the arts should seek to reveal the extra dimensions that the arts bring with them. Should educators go further than this? Should they suggest that any students who do not build a continued attachment to the arts into their lives will be somehow disadvantaging themselves?

There are two issues to be distinguished here. First, the fact that there are goals which we would wish every student to come to possess (as opposed to merely optional goals) does not imply that everyone will weight these goals in the same way. Take civic goals, for instance. In a liberal democracy we expect citizens in general to possess various dispositions to do with the maintenance and promotion of democratic structures. But this does not imply that we expect everyone to become a political activist or even to follow political events. What we *do* expect is quite compatible with encouraging a talented mathematician, say, to devote herself exclusively to mathematics at the expense of following politics, as long as she is aware of the importance of civic involvement and sees that she is facing a conflict of values in which she has regretfully had to give a very low priority to one of them. Engagement in the arts may be seen in the same way as engagement in politics. If there were no place in someone's life for the arts because they were too busy with other work, from this point of view that might be compatible with their still seeing artistic goals as important for themselves but unfortunately having to give them a low, indeed zero, weighting.

The other issue is this. What is to rule out someone's leading a flourishing life and not seeing the arts as *in any way* important for themselves? It is not that they are obliged to weight other things more highly: they simply do not accept the premiss that the arts contribute to their own well-being however much they may contribute to others'. They have other pleasures; they can attain by other routes the self-knowledge, ethical reinforcement and other benefits which the arts provide. They may apply to art in general what Kit Wright (1989) says about poetry:

When they say
That every day
Men die miserably without it
I doubt it.

John White

I do not know of any way in which such people can logically be obliged to think differently – any more than I know of any way in which egoists can be logically obliged to give up their egoism. It may seem to follow from this that educators would be wrong to lead students to believe that they would do well to maintain a continued interest in the arts, since this would be an illicit imposition on them of a view of human well-being which not everyone may share. I find myself torn at this point. The anti-paternalist in me goes along with the point of view just presented; yet I wonder at the same time whether the sceptic who has no place in her life for art is anything more than a philosopher's example and has no counterpart in real life – or, if indeed there are such people, I wonder whether we should not treat them as exceptions whose case should not be allowed to legislate for everyone else. On the latter line of thought, educators can confidently build up in all their students what they hope will be enduring attachments to art, just as they confidently build up lasting dispositions towards altruism, civic involvement, or self-understanding. Perhaps an acceptable compromise between the two positions is to adopt the second, but, so as to minimise the danger of misplaced paternalism, insist that students are made aware at some point of the sceptic's position.

Conclusion

Two aims of arts education have been defended, to do with opening up options and with promoting personal and collective well-being in the further ways specified. These aims apply to *all* students, not just to some. In different ways they show the importance of education in the arts for *anyone's* flourishing, thus providing a justification for compulsory artistic activities in every student's education. There may well be defensible aims which lack this universality. It may, for instance, be a universal aim to encourage commitments which individual students have to activities in which they are especially interested. Within this universal framework will be located aims specific to different individuals: students with an interest in animal welfare will be given guidance in one direction, while those keen on outward bound activities in another. Some students will be encouraged to develop their artistic interests – performing on a musical instrument, drawing and painting, writing plays and stories, ballet dancing, literary criticism. In the context of this paper, I shall make little further reference to such individualised goals, being almost wholly concerned with aims applicable to any learner.

Are the two aims I have suggested exhaustive? Some would say that every child, and not only enthusiasts or those who show a particular talent, should be inducted into the practical arts activities just mentioned: everyone should learn drawing and painting, creative writing, and perhaps also dance, singing or playing an instrument. We have to be careful here to respect the distinction between aims and ways of realising aims. It may be that one way of pursuing the opening-up-options aim is by engaging children in practical arts activities. After all, among the options to which they are to be exposed are things like being a member of an orchestra or writing poetry; and it may seem self-evident that in order to be in an appropriate position to choose such an option one needs experience from within of what it involves. Whether this proposition is indeed self-evident is something to which we will return in the next section. Meanwhile, the point to be made here is that proponents of practical arts activities for all students should make it clear *why* they are advocating them. Do they see them as ways of realising one of the aims we have already discussed, the opening-up-options aim, perhaps? Or do they have some other aim in mind? If so, this needs to be spelt out and defended.

We will be looking in the next section at the place of creative and other practical activities in arts education. Before we turn to this, are there any other defensible aims of a universal sort? Perhaps one such has to do with the aesthetic features of the environment, e.g.. its architecture, urban planning, conservation in town and country, and design of everyday objects. There is a strong argument for encouraging students to care about such matters, in that this should be seen as part of what is involved in being attached to a community, whether national or other. I will leave open whether, beyond this, there are any other valid general aims.

One last thought. *The Arts 5-16* claims, as we have seen, that in the curriculum the arts are equal in importance to mathematics, science or verbal reasoning. It provides no justification for this, and indeed any justification would be hard to provide without specifying in what way 'importance' is to be understood. But the discussion of the two purposes of arts education may throw some light on this. If we are talking about the importance of this pursuit or that for personal flourishing, we have seen several ways in which the arts can make a contribution to this. Most of these have had to do directly with intrinsic rather than extrinsic goals. By contrast mathematics has little direct relevance to intrinsic ends: far fewer people can be expected to spend leisure time pursuing mathematics for its own sake than engaged with the arts; and the contribution of mathematics to self-knowledge and to communal bonding, unlike that of the arts, is remote. The value of mathematics, for all but a few, lies in its extrinsic benefits as a tool for all sorts of useful purposes, often social rather than personal. The same goes for science. Individuals whose education has deprived them of a knowledge of mathematics or science will be disadvantaged to some extent in choosing options, since all sorts of doors, especially to vocations, will be closed to them. But those deprived of the arts may be disbenefited far more than in vocational ways: they will be robbed both of what is generally taken to be one of life's chief joys and also of a rich source of spiritual sustenance.

(B) WAYS OF REALISING AIMS

Both main aims examined in the last section have to do with introducing students to the rich world of the arts, enabling them to derive pleasure and spiritual sustenance from its contemplation. What means best help them to do this?

A simple answer – which may, we shall have to see, prove *too* simple – is that they come to enjoy works of art by enjoying works of art. In the end we expect them to be at home with a wide range of works across all the art forms, to be able to get inside works inaccessible to them earlier, and to perceive new aspects of and layers of significance in works which they have already enjoyed in a less nuanced way. In the beginning this breadth and depth will be lacking: children will engage with works or fragments of work within their capabilities, with *Red Riding Hood*, not *Richard III*. The task of arts educators is to extend outwards from these beginnings, establishing bridgeheads into unknown areas. But all the time the pattern of the advance will be the same, learners' attention being directed, first and last, on to works which other people have created.

There is nothing in this about children's own creative (and other practical) activities or the development of their skills as critics, implying by this an ability to produce public reasoned assessments of the virtues and defects of particular works. In this way the proposal seems to run counter to what I shall call the 'mainstream' view of very many teachers of arts subjects, for whom creative and/or critical activities, as well as sensuous engagement, are of great importance. We saw in our discussion of *The Arts 5-16* that it calls for equal weight to be given to pupil's creative work and to their critical understanding of the work of others. What is meant here by 'critical understanding' is, as we have seen, not wholly clear. It may or may not include sensuous engagement with works, but at all events it seems to go beyond this in the direction of their assessment.

The 'mainstream' view is not necessarily at odds with the 'simple' view that stresses enjoyment of others' works. Art teachers will tell you that encouraging children to draw and paint familiarises them with such things as perspective or contrasts of tone and colour which they can then perceive more adequately in the works of others. Attempting to write one's own poetry, similarly, is said to be an aid to enjoying others'; acquiring the skills of literary criticism, to focus one's attention on features of works which one might otherwise have overlooked.

Claims like these are often taken as self-evidently true. What is not often asked is whether, in so far as the aim of arts education is to cultivate a love of (other people's) art, creative and critical activities are good means of doing this or whether the time spent on them could be more profitably spent on other things. The obvious competitor to them is experience of others' art. Suppose 100 hours in an average 12 year old's annual timetabled time are devoted to practical activities in the arts. What we need to ask is whether spending this time reading literature, looking at pictures, watching films or listening to music – not necessarily during timetabled classes – would do more to develop a feeling for the arts. Prima facie, it seems a reasonable bet that the more direct route will be more reliable. In other fields this is so. In the USSR, at least until recently, learning to drive a car required hours and hours of attendance at lectures on such things as the workings of the internal combustion engine: only towards the end of this theoretical course did learners sit behind the wheel and practise driving. In our own country we take the view that the route to learning to drive is, by and large, driving. The same is true in other areas. One learns to hurdle by hurdling; to think mathematically by thinking mathematically; to become just, as Aristotle first reminded us, by doing just acts. The point is almost so obvious that it is embarrassing to labour it. Yet when it comes to education in the arts it is often ignored. Here, too, however, the presumption must be in favour of the direct route – of developing experience of the arts by encouraging students to experience the arts.

This is only a presumption. It *may* be the case that a certain amount of engagement in creative and critical activities is a most helpful means to this end. But if so, the case has to be made: we cannot leave matters to the received opinion of practitioners. It would not be enough for them to point to instances of pupils who through their own practical activities in art and music have gone on to enjoy Van Gogh and Mozart. There are indeed such cases. The real issue is larger-scale. We are talking not about talented children only but about *all* our young people and how best they may come to love the arts. Evidence in favour of practical activities will have to be more substantial than that.

There are, in any case, reasons to think that in some contexts they may be counterproductive. The common practice of sitting a class down and asking them to paint a picture or write a poem on a theme that captures their imagination may help to give them a misleading picture of how artists proceed. These do not create their works on a word of command; they do not expect to be able to turn something out at 11.20 every Tuesday morning; they do not work with a roomful of other artists. And since, as in any good classroom, the children will be rewarded with a good deal of praise for their achievements, they may come to see art-making as easier than it is. Nothing in their experience of the art-room or the English lesson may reveal to them the technical difficulties which artists have to overcome and also the comparative rarity and uncontrollability of such creativeness. Making a collage or working with their class to compose a simple piece of music will not teach them about the waywardness of inspiration, about despair and self-doubt, about the constraints and benefits of traditional forms or their transcendence, about belonging to a fraternity of fellow-artists. The concept of art they are acquiring may come to connote fun, plain sailing, masses of positive feedback. If they are particularly successful and go on from strength to strength, they may be developing dispositions not of humility and reverence before outstanding achievements, but of vanity.

Mainstreamers may reply that these dangers are avoidable by sensible teaching. Students will not be spending all their time on their own creations: they will also be studying the lives of artists and their works. I have seen excellent examples of teaching of this kind, but how widespread it is I do not know. Yet even where it exists, the question still remains: could the time spent on creative activities be put to better use?

Critical activities may also lead students away from the desired goal. They may build up inappropriate dispositions towards, say, reading literature. Students may become too ratiocinative towards it, too intent on finding contrasts of characterisation or unexpected enjambements to be fully absorbed in the magic of a work, to be captivated by its vividness or wit. They may become altogether too active in their stance towards it, not allowing it to take them over, to seduce them into a dreamy contemplation of it. Once again we will be told that criticism need not have this undesirable effect and that a good teacher will use it to enhance, not to detract from, one's enjoyment of a work. This is no doubt true. But at the same time we all know of people whose attitudes to literature have been warped by their experience of analysing texts for public examinations: they carry with them from those times an uneasy sense of obligation, a feeling that they have to approach a novel or poem in an approved way, that they have to show publicly that they possess the requisite sensitivity to its aesthetic qualities.

One answer that mainstreamers will give to the 'direct' proposal that the best way of fostering a love of art may be by the route of sensuous engagement is that this does not fit the psychology of children. We cannot imagine art or music lessons from age five upwards devoted exclusively to looking at paintings or listening to music. Children want to be active. They need to get their hands on paintbrushes and drumsticks.

But this begs the question. If young children cannot get very far in enjoying music or painting, it does not follow that they must be given something more active in the same areas. An alternative is not to give them art or music classes at all. There is no evidence that I know to show that the best way of fostering a love of these arts is to make classes in them compulsory from five to sixteen. I am aware that the 1988 National Curriculum did just this, but would hardly see it as a reliable model to follow, since in this major recommendation as in most of its others, it gave no reasons whatsoever in favour of its adoption. If a love of music and painting typically comes, if at all, with adolescence, then it might, for all I know, be better to wait until then to promote it. In saying this, I am not laying down categorically that this *would* be the best thing to do: it is rather that I don't know, and I don't think anyone else knows, how best to generate a love of the arts. We need to explore all promising hypotheses.

In any case, we need not assume that the best way of attaining this end is by spreading curricular attention *across all the arts* in every year of schooling. For all we know – and again we must wait on evidence – some students, perhaps even all students, may most easily gain access to the whole world of the arts via their experience of one or two particular arts. For many people an acquaintance with literature, say, plus perhaps film, may be a good entree to music or painting.

Prima facie this particular suggestion may well be worth following up in planning the curriculum. The psychological objection to confronting young children with paintings and pieces of music evaporates when we turn to literature or film. Show a seven year old pictures in frames – as distinct, say, from book illustrations – and he may quickly grow bored. But every seven year old loves listening to, watching or reading stories. Educators have an obvious foundation on which to build. Children can go on to longer, more complicated, more demanding stories. With the years they can not only gain pleasure and deeper benefits from literature and film, they can also begin to acquire sensitivity to general aesthetic values – unity, complexity, delicacy, expressiveness – transferable to some extent to works in other media.

This is only one suggestion. I am not advocating it as the best way forward, only using it to help free us from the cramp of conventional attitudes. We need to dream up all sorts of possible new approaches. In this, too, we should not be too fixated on timetabled activities. Since the time when English, music and art lessons entered the curriculum well over a century ago, the possibilities for education in these and other arts have been immeasurably transformed by the coming of radio, film, television, recording and the advances made in graphic art and design. We can no longer, if we ever could, take as our starting point the traditional subjects of the timetabled curriculum, or even what might take place in schools on a somewhat wider canvas. Once again, we need to go back to our central objectives: to promote a love of the arts and provide a solid basis for choice in this area. In considering how these aims may best be achieved we need to look at the contribution the media can make, including the central role of the home in shaping children's media experiences, and bridges that can be built from more popular and accessible forms of art available through the media like pop songs, films and soap operas to more demanding and many-layered works. The school can have all sorts of roles in making links with home and in building these bridges; but it can probably no longer be the main vehicle of arts education, and its ways of organising its work within traditional subject-barriers need urgently to be reviewed.

Yet what I have called mainstream attitudes are still very strong, entrenched within the subject-based structures of the teaching profession and teacher education. So far in this section I have been assuming that mainstreamers share the overarching goals of the last section to do with sensuous engagement, and that they argue only that creative and/or critical activities in school are good ways of trying to realise them. My conclusion so far has been that while this may be so, we should not assume that it is but wait on evidence. Certainly any stronger claim to the effect that creative activities are *necessary* to a love of art, is vulnerable to obvious counterinstances: there are plenty of lovers of poetry who have never written verse; and there must be few actual cathedral builders in the ranks of those who marvel at Lincoln or Canterbury. But even the weaker claim, that creative pursuits are *helpful*, is by no means to be taken for granted, as we have seen.

The place of creative and critical activities in schools needs reassessment. Not all their advocates, in any case, would lay the same emphasis that I have done on love of art as a central objective. Many practitioners see their main task as unlocking the student's own creative potential, either for its own sake or as a means of bringing about a more general liberation. This is not the place to go into a full-scale critique of the luxuriant psychological and educational theories that abound in this area, partly because the job has already been done by such writers as Dearden (1968, esp. ch. 7) and Abbs (1987). I will restrict myself to the more general observation that advocates of compulsory creative and critical activities need to be clear about the grounds on which they rely and non-partisan in their assessment. Many of these grounds may be valid, but these need to be winnowed from those which are not and their relation to the larger picture of educational aims needs to be spelt out. Creative activities are often favoured, for instance, because they give students experience in practical problem-solving or because they enable them to work co-operatively together. These seem to me fine objectives and may well justify the time a school devotes to creative work, but they need have nothing to do with promoting a love of art.

I must underline again that in all these comments about practical art I have been talking only about *compulsory* activities. It is quite compatible with this to say that there should be extensive opportunities for students to paint, draw, sing, play musical instruments on an optional or voluntary basis. Many children enjoy doing these things and they should be allowed plenty of scope to do so. Too many school activities are now compulsory, intended for everybody. We need to be more careful than we are in laying down what should be compulsory for all and oblige children to participate only in those things which can be justified in a universal way. If practical art *can* be so justified, whether as a gateway to a love of art or in some other way, then it can have a place in the compulsory curriculum; if not, its role is still assured, but in a non-compulsory system. We would do well, as I argued nearly twenty years ago in *Towards a Compulsory Curriculum* (White, 1973), to pare down the compulsory part of the school day to a justifiable minimum and in the time saved to arrange all sorts of options from which students can select. In any such system practical art activities would be likely to be popular choices.

CONCLUSION

Education in the arts, as it exists in British schools today, lacks a coherent sense of purpose. This is partly because until very recently the arts have not been considered as a whole, but have been rigidly pigeonholed, largely into English, music and art; and partly because the British have traditionally been weak in setting out clear aims for areas of educational content, not only in the arts, but across the board. The *Arts 5-16* project, following the lead of the Gulbenkian Report, has had a bold first shot at an integrated policy. But its approach is too simplistic and pays insufficient attention to underlying aims. In the second part of this paper I have sought to lay the foundation for a more adequate alternative. Most of this has been about aims, since this is the proper place at which to begin. There is much more to be said not only about aims, but also about ways of realising them. Important questions remain about how, even assuming we could all reach a broad consensus on ends and means, present arrangements in schools could be modified accordingly. I do not want to underestimate the difficulties here. Subject-confined attitudes and modi operandi that have been with us for up to a century will be hard to change. But that is no reason for not trying to change them if we know there is a better way forward.

POSTSCRIPT, JANUARY 1992

The paper has concentrated on the arts in schools in general, not on specific subjects like art, music and literature. What place these should have in the whole picture is only to be determined once the latter is sketched in outline. But at the time when this paper is about to go to press in January 1992, public controversy has erupted over the National Curriculum Council's response to the recommendations of the working groups on Art and on Music. It seems appropriate to say a few words about this.

The NCC's response has been to cut down the number of attainment targets in each subject from three to two, thus giving somewhat more weighting to 'knowledge and understanding' than to practical objectives to do with making art or performing and composing music. It recommends from an early age acquaintance with and ability to comment on the work of well-known artists and composers within the Western tradition.

Dispute has already erupted over whether it is sensible to expect seven-year olds to listen and talk about pieces of music by Mozart and Stravinsky, as well as over the role of practical activities and of non-western art and music in the curriculum. It is likely to continue. But both the major contestants in these debates, that is, those who support the more catholic approach of the working parties and the 'traditionalists', take as read that art and music ought to be compulsory subjects for all children from age 5 to at least age 14. But no justification for this assumption has yet been given. It was part of the framework of the overall National Curriculum introduced by Kenneth Baker in 1987 and enshrined in law in the 1988 Education Reform Act. This framework was presented without any rationale and none has been given since.

The assumption needs to be questioned. Whatever aims are mooted for arts education 5-16 taken as a whole – that is, whether the aims suggested in this paper about promoting a love of the arts are accepted or others are proposed in their place – the question how those aims are to be realised in curricular arrangements is *secondary*. Until we have the general aims clear we cannot say whether they are best promoted by having separate lessons in music, visual and other arts, or – and this is most important – whether all the main art forms need to be represented in the curriculum for all those nine years. It may be better, for all we know now, not to begin a systematic introduction to music or the visual arts until age eleven, or even later.

In accepting the assumption, both sides, traditionalists and non-traditionalists, face the problem of how all those curriculum slots are to be filled for one hour a week or more throughout all those nine years. Some want to pack them more with acquiring knowledge about artists, others with more varied activities. But does all this time need to be spent? It should be taken as a central principle of curriculum planning that time should not be allotted for compulsory classes unless there are good reasons for this. Obliging children to do art and/or music from the age of five may even, for all we know, help to put them off these subjects in later life rather than encourage them towards them. It may be, again for all we know, that the optimum time to begin this work is after fourteen, just at the age when, in line with Kenneth Clarke's recent fiat, art and music are no longer to be compulsory.

This last thought deserves further consideration. For how many others besides myself have the worlds of music, painting, sculpture and architecture burst into our consciousness with the new emotions, energies, yearnings and perplexities of adolescence? How far should those concerned with art and music in education be directing their attention not to hammering out what should fill all those curricular slots from the reception class upwards, but to pressing for more adequate provision for the 14-19 age-range?

John White

NOTE

Part of the material in Part II will also appear in R Barrow and P A White, eds. *Aspects of Liberal Education*, Routledge, forthcoming.

REFERENCES

Reports

Calouste Gulbenkian Foundation, 1982. *The arts in schools: Principles, practice and provision*, Gulbenkian Foundation.

HMI, 1977. *Curriculum 11-16*, London, Department of Education and Science.

National Curriculum Council, 1990. *The Arts 5-16: A curriculum framework*, Harlow, Oliver and Boyd.

Other works

Abbs, P, 1987. 'Towards a coherent arts aesthetic' in Abbs, P., ed. *Living powers: The arts in education*, London, Falmer.

Dearden, R F, 1968. *The philosophy of primary education*, London, Routledge and Kegan Paul.

Dearden, R F, 1984, *Theory and practice in education*, London, Routledge and Kegan Paul.

Elliott, R K, 1972. 'Aesthetic theory and the experience of art' in Osborne, H., ed. *Aesthetics*, Oxford University Press.

Hamlyn, D W, 1977. 'Self knowledge' in Mischel, T. ed. *The self*, Oxford, Blackwell.

Hirst, P H, 1965. 'Liberal education and the nature of knowledge' in Archambault, R. D., ed. *Philosophical analysis and education*, London, Routledge and Kegan Paul.

MacIntyre, A, 1981. *After virtue*, London, Duckworth.

O'Hear, A, 1988. *The element of fire*, London, Routledge.

Osborne, H, 1986. Review of H B Redfern Questions in aesthetic education, *Journal of Philosophy of Education* Vol 20 No 2.

Passmore, J, 1970. *The perfectibility of man*, London, Duckworth.

Savile, A, 1982. *The test of time*, Oxford, Clarendon Press.

Taylor, C, 1990. *The sources of the self*, Cambridge University Press.

White, J P, 1973. *Towards a compulsory curriculum*, London, Routledge and Kegan Paul.

Williams, B, 1985. *Ethics and the limits of philosophy*, London, Fontana.

Wright K, 1989. 'Poetry' in his *Short afternoons*, London, Hutchinson.

MORE HAS MEANT WOMEN: THE FEMINISATION OF SCHOOLING

Jane Miller

'To an extent that is quite inadequately recognised, state education is provided by women; as is virtually all schooling, whether public or private, for young children.' Jane Miller argues that criticism of current educational practice often has gender as its hidden target. She draws on historical evidence and on her own teaching experience to develop a complex and provocative discussion.

WHAT WE KNOW ABOUT EFFECTIVE PRIMARY TEACHING

Caroline Gipps

Caroline Gipps looks at the findings of research and educational theorists on what are the most effective classroom practices and teaching methods in the primary school. Primary teachers faced with the introduction of the National Curriculum and related assessment, and calls from government ministers and others to move back to more formal methods in the classroom, will find here much to stimulate an examination of their practice, as well as encouragement to see the value and potential of their work.

MUSIC EDUCATION AND THE NATIONAL CURRICULUM

Keith Swanwick

Keith Swanwick discusses the evolution of music education in schools and critically examines the implications of the attainment targets in the National Curriculum. On the central question of music as knowledge he considers that the National Curriculum Working Group put a misplaced emphasis on factual information and quantity. Knowing about and understanding music is much more than processing factual information and any form of assessment must recognise *qualitative* awareness rather than acquisition of *quantitative* facts. Swanwick's improved criteria for assessment have in part been accepted by the Secretary of State for Education. In this strongly argued work Swanwick seeks to identify a way forward for music in the classroom that would secure the confidence of musicians and music educators.

SCHOOL HISTORY TEACHING: Has the National Curriculum got it right?

Peter Lee, John Slater, Paddy Walsh and John White

The coming of the National Curriculum has left many questions unresolved about the aims of school history teaching and how these cohere with the aims of schools in general. Certain issues have attracted public attention, such as the weight to be given to British, as distinct from world, history, the relative weight to be given to learning the facts of history and to a broader understanding, and whether history should be optional after 14. But underlying these are deeper considerations. Why study history in school at all? Is it something to be engaged in for its own sake, or as part of education for citizenship? Is it just an expression of piety towards the past? Answers to such questions will determine attitudes towards and the content of history in the National Curriculum. The contributors to this London File paper - historians and philosophers - try to come to grips with these questions and comment on each other's views. The arguments and conclusions have important implications for the future of school history.

THE RIGHTS OF THE CHILD: Educational implications of the United Nations Convention

Susan Wolfson

The United Nations Convention on the Rights of the Child has profound and exciting implications for change in general educational ethos as well as for concrete educational reforms. Susan Wolfson discusses the ideological background to the Convention, the arguments on all sides of children's rights issues, and the correct balancing of those rights with states' responsibilities and parental entitlements. She examines the rights which children are denied by current educational practice, measuring them against the Convention's specifications article by article. She concludes that legal reforms as well as educational policy and practice changes must occur for states, parents and educationalists to fulfil their new responsibilities within the Convention, and for children fully to realize their new status within educational institutions and in their larger lives.

THE PROMISE AND PERILS OF EDUCATIONAL COMPARISON

Martin McLean

Education in other countries was rediscovered by government in Britain in the mid-1980s, after almost a century of neglect. Policy makers have made unprecedented appeals to foreign - apparently more successful - practice to support new policies. Does this reflect a new global order in which educational institutions must compete with international rivals just as fiercely as car manufacturers? Or is it a search for instant certainties in a world bereft of utopias, where everything is compared - students, teachers, schools, localities, countries and historical epochs - against slippery or specious norms? Martin McLean discusses the purposes, techniques and possibilities of cross-national educational comparison. He analyses international surveys of student attainment and of vocational education and the reports of the first twelve HMI expeditions to other systems. He argues that, properly done, comparison can enrich British education policy, but that, in too many cases, it has produced deceptive evidence which few have the means to check.

CHARTERS, CHOICES AND EDUCATIONAL RESPONSIBILITIES

Anthony Green

Anthony Green looks at the Citizen's Charter and the Parent's Charter, both issued by the Government in 1991. The 'charters' are political documents designed to appeal to voters, but they could well serve as the basis for legislation to come. They are also significant in their own terms as statements about rights and responsibilities in education. Central to them are the notions of informed choice, the restructuring of professional-client relations and 'value for money', as well as specification of parental rights and responsibilities. Anthony Green's aim is to present an analysis of the social, civil and political rights the charters seem to imply, and to develop discussion of the educational entitlements they endorse, deny and obscure.

SCHOOL HISTORY TEACHING: HAS THE NATIONAL CURRICULUM GOT IT RIGHT?

Peter Lee, John Slater, Paddy Walsh and John White

The coming of the National Curriculum has left unresolved questions about the aims of school history teaching and how these cohere with the aims of schools in general. Certain issues have attracted public attention; the weight to be given to British, as distinct from world, history, the relative weight to be given to learning the facts of history and to a broader understanding, and whether history should be optional after 14. But underlying these are deeper considerations. Why study history in school at all? Is it something to be engaged in for its own sake, or as part of education for citizenship? Is it just an expression of piety towards the past? Answers to such questions will determine attitudes towards and the content of history in the National Curriculum. The contributors to this London File paper - historians and philosophers - try to come to grips with these questions. Their arguments and conclusions have important implications for the future of school history.

For a full list of the London File Papers please write to
THE TUFNELL PRESS,
47 DALMENY ROAD,
LONDON,
N7 0DY